Where Does It Come From?

From Vine to Pizza

by Penelope S. Nelson

Bullfrog Books

Ideas for Parents and Teachers

Bullfrog Books let children practice reading informational text at the earliest reading levels. Repetition, familiar words, and photo labels support early readers.

Before Reading

- Discuss the cover photo. What does it tell them?

- Look at the picture glossary together. Read and discuss the words.

Read the Book

- "Walk" through the book and look at the photos. Let the child ask questions. Point out the photo labels.

- Read the book to the child, or have him or her read independently.

After Reading

- Prompt the child to think more. Ask: Have you ever made a homemade pizza? What did you put on it?

Bullfrog Books are published by Jump!
5357 Penn Avenue South
Minneapolis, MN 55419
www.jumplibrary.com

Library of Congress Cataloging-in-Publication Data

Names: Nelson, Penelope, 1994– author.
Title: From vine to pizza / Penelope S. Nelson.
Description: Minneapolis, MN: Jump!, Inc., [2021]
Series: Where does it come from?
Audience: Ages 5–8.
Audience: Grades K–1.
Identifiers: LCCN 2019055094 (print)
LCCN 2019055095 (ebook)
ISBN 9781645275411 (library binding)
ISBN 9781645275428 (paperback)
ISBN 9781645275435 (ebook)
Subjects: LCSH: Tomatoes—Juvenile literature.
Tomato sauces—Juvenile literature.
Pizza—Juvenile literature.
Classification: LCC SB349 .N44 2021 (print)
LCC SB349 (ebook) | DDC 635/.642—dc23
LC record available at https://lccn.loc.gov/2019055094
LC ebook record available at https://lccn.loc.gov/2019055095

Editor: Jenna Gleisner
Designer: Anna Peterson

Photo Credits: Iurii Kachkovskyi/Shutterstock, cover (left); stockcreations/Shutterstock, cover (right); Zigzag Mountain Art/Shutterstock, 1, 18–19, 22bm; Maks Narodenko/Shutterstock, 3; StockImageFactory.com/Shutterstock, 4; Kwangmoozaa/Shutterstock, 5, 22tl, 23br; Volkova/Shutterstock, 6–7; Nick David/Getty, 8–9; Shutterstock, 10–11, 12, 23tr; arrideo/Shutterstock, 13, 22tr, 23tl; Rimma _ Bondarenko/iStock, 14–15, 23bl; BW Folsom/Shutterstock, 16, 22br; Nagy-Bagoly Arpad/Shutterstock, 17; glenda/Shutterstock, 20–21, 22bl; Brenda Carson/Shutterstock, 24.

Printed in the United States of America at Corporate Graphics in North Mankato, Minnesota.

Table of Contents

Red Sauce

Max loves pizza!
Where does
the sauce
come from?

tomato

vine

Tomatoes!
They grow on vines.

They are made
into sauce!

Where?

Sauce is made
in factories.

We can make it at home, too!

How?

First, we cut the tomatoes.

Onions add flavor.
Garlic does, too.
We put them
in a pan.

onion

pan

garlic

13

We add the tomatoes!

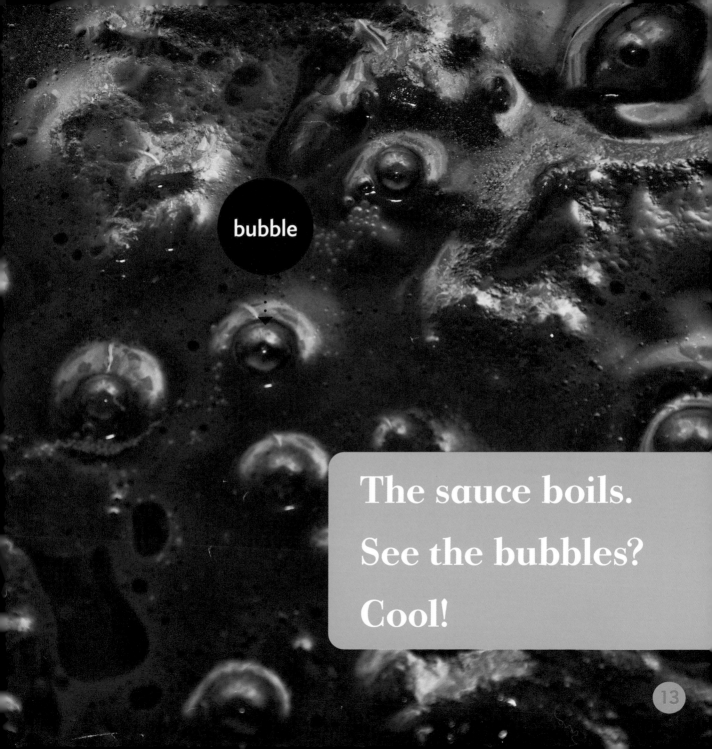

bubble

The sauce boils.
See the bubbles?
Cool!

basil

We add herbs.
Basil is one.

We let it cook.

It gets thicker.

Mac tastes it.
Yum!

We put it in jars.

We can eat it later!

jar

We make pizza!
Sauce goes on first.
Jo adds cheese.
Yum!

21

From Vine to Table

How are tomatoes made into sauce and then used to make pizza?

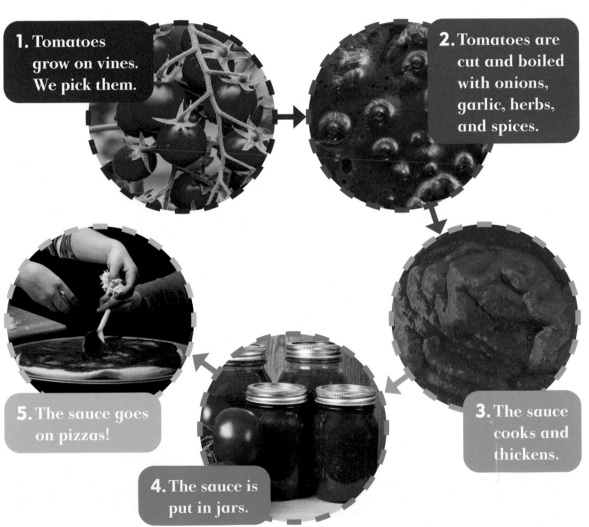

1. Tomatoes grow on vines. We pick them.

2. Tomatoes are cut and boiled with onions, garlic, herbs, and spices.

3. The sauce cooks and thickens.

4. The sauce is put in jars.

5. The sauce goes on pizzas!

Picture Glossary

boils
Heats to the point where
it bubbles.

flavor
Taste.

herbs
Plants or plant parts that are
used in cooking to add flavor.

vines
Plants with long, twining
stems that grow along the
ground or climb.

Index

To Learn More

Finding more information is as easy as 1, 2, 3.

❶ Go to www.factsurfer.com

❷ Enter "fromvinetopizza" into the search box.

❸ Choose your book to see a list of websites.